PIANO . VOCAL . GUITAR

SAM SMITH   THE THRILL OF IT ALL

ISBN 978-1-5400-1567-9

7777 W. BLUEMOUND RD. P.O. BOX 13819 MILWAUKEE, WI 53213

In Australia Contact:
Hal Leonard Australia Pty. Ltd.
4 Lentara Court
Cheltenham, Victoria, 3192 Australia
Email: ausadmin@halleonard.com.au

Visit Hal Leonard Online at
www.halleonard.com

TOO GOOD AT GOODBYES

Words and Music by SAM SMITH,
TOR HERMANSEN, MIKKEL ERIKSEN
and JAMES NAPIER

Pop Ballad

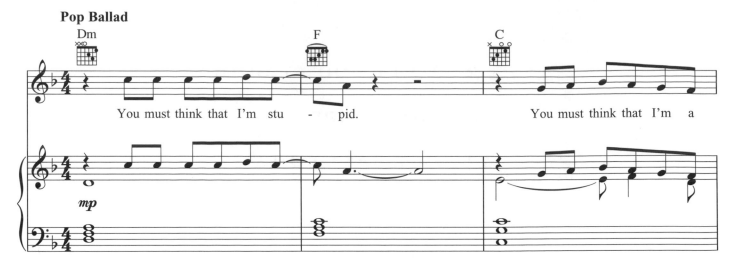

You must think that I'm stu - pid. You must think that I'm a

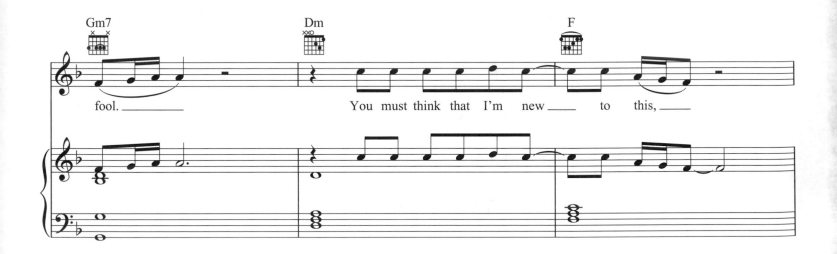

fool. You must think that I'm new ___ to this, ___

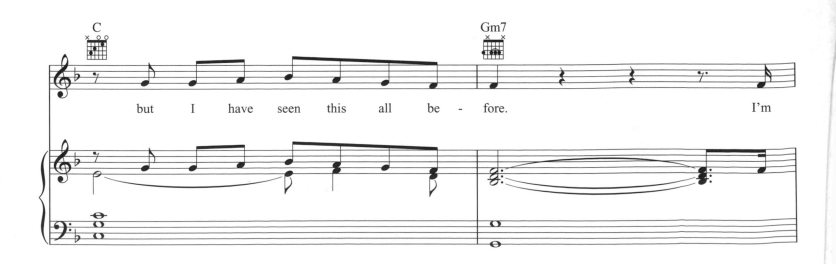

but I have seen this all be - fore. I'm

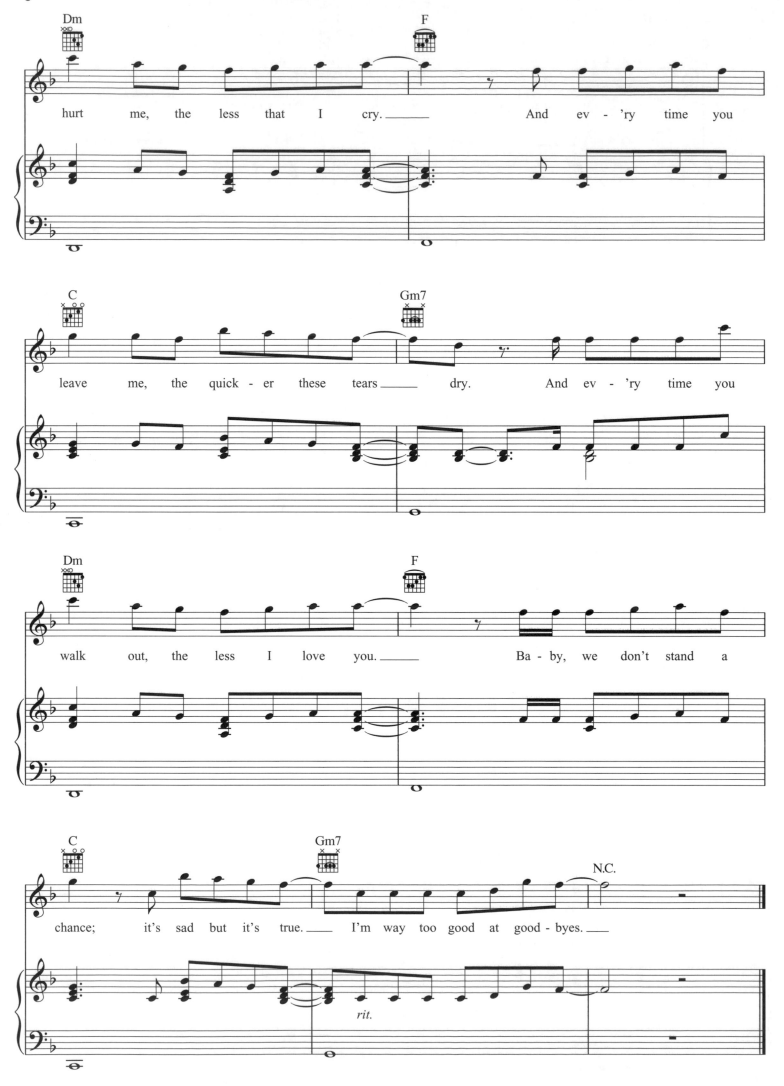

SAY IT FIRST

Words and Music by SAM SMITH,
JAMES NAPIER and JAMES RYAN WUIHUN HO

MIDNIGHT TRAIN

Words and Music by SAM SMITH,
JAMES NAPIER and JAMES RYAN WUIHUN HO

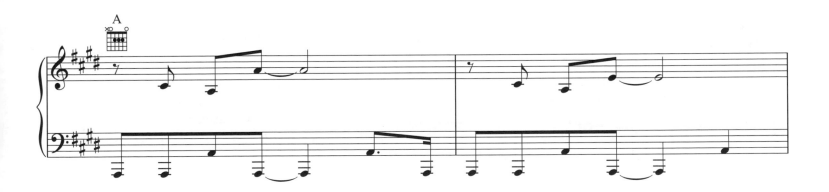

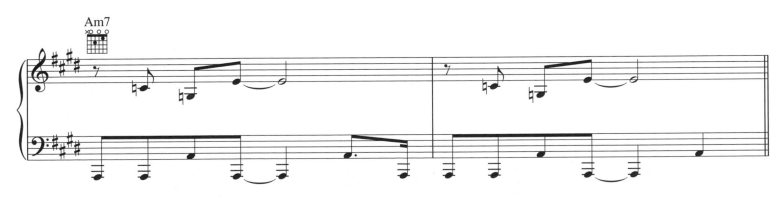

Ba ba do. Ba ba do. _____

D.S. al Coda

_____ to walk _____ a - way. _____ Can't stop cry - ing,

I hate that I've caused you _____ pain. _____ But I can't de - ny it,

So I pick up the piec - es, get on the mid - night __ train. __ I've got my rea - sons

but dar - ling, I can't ex - plain. __ I'll al - ways __ love you but to - night's _

___ the night _____ I choose __ to walk __ a - way. _____

ONE LAST SONG

Words and Music by SAM SMITH,
JAMES NAPIER, TYLER JOHNSON
and CHARLES EMANUEL SMALLS

* *Recorded a half step lower.*
** *Male vocals written at pitch.*

HIM

Words and Music by SAM SMITH,
BRENDAN GRIEVE and REUBEN JAMES

Piano Ballad

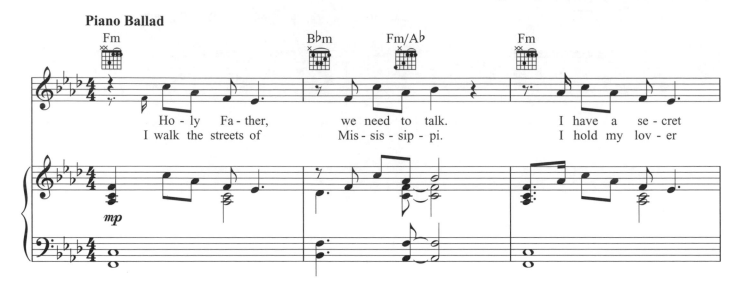

Ho - ly Fa - ther, we need to talk. I have a se - cret
I walk the streets of Mis - sis - sip - pi. I hold my lov - er

that I can't ___ keep. I'm not the boy ___ that
by the ___ hand. I feel you star - ing

you thought you want - ed. Please don't get an - gry,
when he is with ___ me. How can I make ___ you

BURNING

Words and Music by SAM SMITH,
JASON BOYD, DOMINIC JORDAN
and JIMMY GIANNOS

Recorded a half step higher.

BABY, YOU MAKE ME CRAZY

Words and Music by SAM SMITH, JAMES NAPIER, EMILE HAYNIE,
DENNIS THOMAS, WOODROW SPARROW, GENE REDD SR.,
GEORGE BROWN, CLAYDES SMITH, RICHARD WESTFIELD,
ROBERT BELL, ROBERT MICKENS and RONALD BELL

NO PEACE

Words and Music by SAM SMITH,
JAMES NAPIER and ABBEY SMITH

Will you give ___ me the piece, __ will you give __ me the piece __ of my heart? __

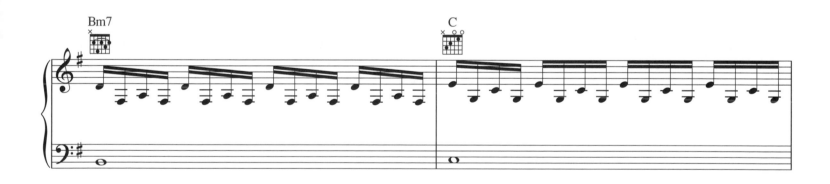

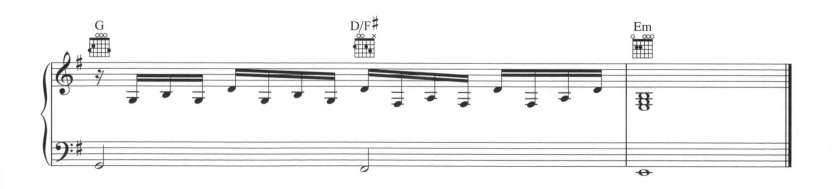

PRAY

Words and Music by SAM SMITH,
JAMES NAPIER, TIM MOSLEY,
JOSÉ VELASQUEZ and LARRANCE DOPSON

PALACE

Words and Music by SAM SMITH,
CAMARON OCHS and TYLER JOHNSON

NOTHING LEFT FOR YOU

Words and Music by SAM SMITH
and JAMES NAPIER

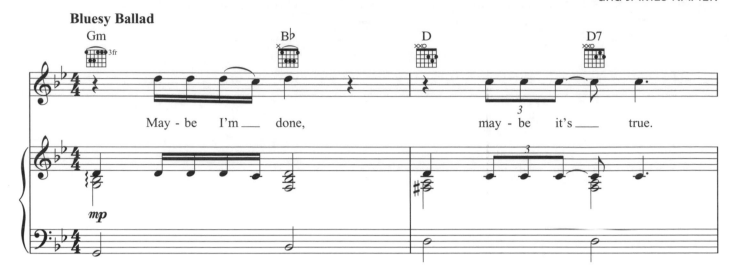

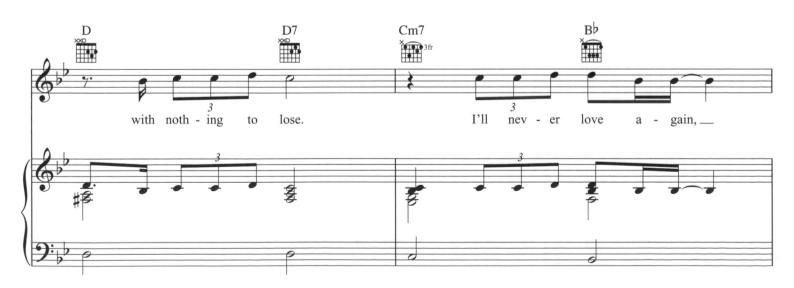

THE THRILL OF IT ALL

Words and Music by SAM SMITH,
BRENDAN GRIEVE and REUBEN JAMES

SCARS

Words and Music by SAM SMITH
and BRENDAN GRIEVE

Moderately Slow

This is for my moth-er from the old-er broth-er of your chil-dren, made of three. Now you
This is for my fa-ther from the old-er broth-er of your chil-dren, made of three. Yeah, you've

found your lov-er 'cause it was-n't our fa-ther who made you laugh and hap-py. It's been a
been so good to us and showed us how to live and taught us to be free. But when

long five years, I've cried a thou-sand tears, and here we are af-ter the war. But we're
Moth-er told you that she did-n't love you, all these bridg-es hit the sea. So you

ONE DAY AT A TIME

Words and Music by SAM SMITH
and SIMON ALDRED

Gentle Acoustic Ballad

Let's turn off our phones __ to-night __ and re-ly __ on the stars. __
I know you're feel-ing weighed down __ to-night __ and you can't __ find the breaks. __

We've been so lost __ late-ly, we for-got who we __ are.
Ev-'ry day is too long for you, you are sworn to your __ fate. __

* Recorded a half-step higher

But I got ev-'ry-thing I need, ba-by, in the palms of your touch. ___ In a
But we got ev-'ry-thing we need, ba-by, in the mem-'ries we make. ___ In a

world of dark dis-trac-tions, it can all get too much.}
world of re-in-ven-tions, it's ___ nev-er too late.} So let's sit by an

Eng-lish ___ riv-er 'til the wa-ter runs dry. ___

Can we light a cig-a-rette and talk a-bout days ___ gone by? We're nei-ther

saints or — sin-ners _____ so leave your his-t'ry be-hind. _____ Let's

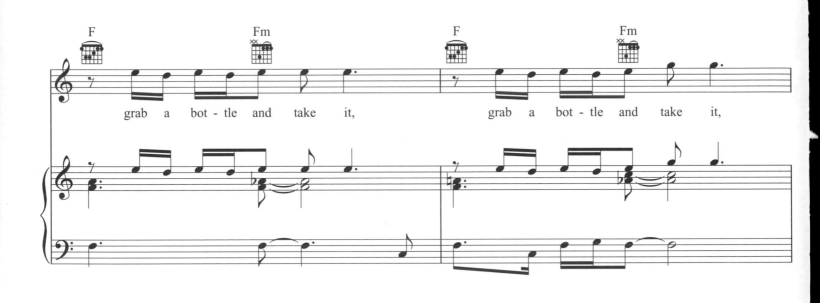

grab a bot-tle and take it, grab a bot-tle and take it,

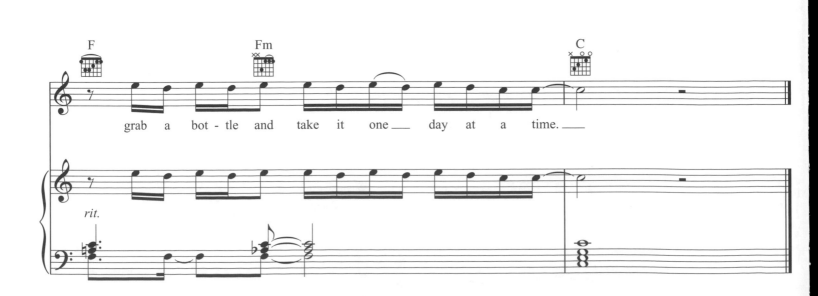

grab a bot-tle and take it one__ day at a time.__